T0151161

Selfie

Selfie

Christine Quintana

Playwrights Canada Press
Toronto

For professional or amateur production rights, please contact:
Colin Rivers, Marquis Entertainment
312-73 Richmond St. W., Toronto, ON M5H 4E8
416.960.9123, info@marquisent.ca, www.marquisent.ca

LIBRARY AND ARCHIVES CANADA CATALOGUING IN PUBLICATION
Title: Selfie / Christine Quintana.
Names: Quintana, Christine, author.
Description: First edition. | A play.
Identifiers: Canadiana (print) 20200352245 | Canadiana (ebook) 20200352253 | ISBN 9780369101259 (softcover) | ISBN 9780369101266 (PDF) | ISBN 9780369101273 (EPUB) | ISBN 9780369101280 (Kindle)
Classification: LCC PS8633.U5835 S45 2020 | DDC C812/.6—dc23

Playwrights Canada Press operates on Mississaugas of the Credit, Wendat, Anishinaabe, Métis, and Haudenosaunee land. It always was and always will be Indigenous land.

We acknowledge the financial support of the Canada Council for the Arts—which last year invested $153 million to bring the arts to Canadians throughout the country—the Ontario Arts Council (OAC), Ontario Creates, and the Government of Canada for our publishing activities.

Canada Council
for the Arts

Conseil des arts
du Canada

ONTARIO ARTS COUNCIL
CONSEIL DES ARTS DE L'ONTARIO
an Ontario government agency
un organisme du gouvernement de l'Ontario

To anyone waiting for the surface to break.

Selfie was originally commissioned as part of Théâtre la Seizième's dramaturgical development program, and premiered in French in April 2015 in Vancouver.

The play was commissioned and dramaturged for the premiere English production by Young People's Theatre, Toronto, from April 23 to May 11, 2018, with the following cast and creative team:

Chris: Christopher Allen
Emma: Rachel Mutombo
Lily: Caroline Toal

Director and Dramaturg: Stephen Colella
Set and Costume Design: Claire Hill
Lighting Design: Oz Weaver
Sound Design: Deanna Choi
Video Design: Daniel Oulton
Stage Manager: Katerina Sokyrko

A Note on Casting

When casting *Selfie*, I strongly encourage you to take care that the cast on stage reflects the populations and intersections of high school students where you live.

With that said, this word of advice—there is no such thing as colour-blind casting.

Why?

Because the policing system in Canada is not colour blind. Because the medical system in Canada is not colour blind. Because the education system in Canada is not colour blind. Because the justice system in Canada is not colour blind.

Without changing a word of the text, the way Black actors, Indigenous actors, and POC actors are cast in this show can drastically change the stakes and context of the scenes. The real-life consequences of these fictional scenarios are real, are visible to artists and audiences, and need to be honoured.

If you feel like you cannot have a conversation with your artists about how race and gender intersect in your production of *Selfie*, you are likely not prepared to do this work. This play asks a lot of the artists who embody the characters, particularly those who are racialized in a Canadian context. These realities require space, time, and care to be fully realized in the context of the play.

At its core, *Selfie* is about the loving and loyal relationships between the three characters. That aspect of this piece will not change. The way their lives are affected by the power structures around them, however, will change. Honour the experiences of your community by letting those systemic injustices be alive in the work, and by empowering the artists in your community to bring their full selves to wherever they find this piece.

A Note on Social Media

This is not a play about social media any more than *Romeo and Juliet* is a play about letters. It's a medium for communication, but it is not the antagonist or the social issue.

Even in the course of this play's development, the apps mentioned and their functions have changed and shifted to stay current. I encourage you to do so with this script until it can no longer be updated and *Selfie* reaches the natural point at which it will become a period piece (as our digital half-life makes new little epochs with every iOS update).

Notes on the Text

Slashes (/) indicate the spot where the next spoken line should begin.

Beats are just a breath (there's not a lot of time for that otherwise).

Pauses are a change in thought, or the search for something to say, and are sometimes painfully long.

Characters

Emma
Sixteen years old. Thoughtful and intuitive.

Lily
Sixteen years old. Emma's best friend. Big heart and big mouth.

Chris
Seventeen years old. Lily's big brother. A good guy.

Scene 1

The Rules

They address the audience. Behind them, large screens illuminate their descriptions.

LILY: Okay

CHRIS: Okay

EMMA: Okay

LILY / EMMA / CHRIS: SO

LILY: Let's say there's three versions of you

CHRIS: The one everyone thinks you are

EMMA: The one you wished you really were

LILY: And the real you. Whatever that means

EMMA: And take any person

CHRIS: Your sister

LILY: Your best friend

EMMA: Your uh ... friend

CHRIS: Which version of them do you know?

LILY: Which version of them do they give you?

EMMA: And how can you tell?

LILY: OKAY, so take the Insta test

CHRIS: Lily loves the Instagram test

EMMA: She says you can tell everything you need to about someone by looking at their pics

LILY: What do they put out there?

EMMA: What do they want people to see?

CHRIS: What do they want to hide?

LILY: Take Emma

CHRIS: Lily

EMMA: Chris

CHRIS / EMMA / LILY: Well

LILY: Emma used to always make a goofy face in pictures

EMMA: Chris doesn't have to take selfies, because there's always someone taking a photo of him

SELFIE

CHRIS: I'm pretty sure Lily only posts selfies

LILY: Look! In every pic, she's trying to hide

EMMA: Every photo has a bunch of people in it

CHRIS: Every photo: duckface. That's the face she makes when she's jacking the bathroom mirror for an hour every morning

LILY: But this summer, she suddenly became a babe

CHRIS: Mom would kill her if she saw this one

EMMA: Here he is with a bunch of girls in crop tops. Here he is with the soccer team

LILY: Emma 2.0

EMMA: But it feels like something is missing

CHRIS: The guys on my team love her—

LILY: Is she still the same on the inside?

EMMA: Is that who he really is?

CHRIS: But do they actually know her?

LILY: So that's Emma

CHRIS: Lily

EMMA: Chris

LILY: And if that's all you saw, what would you think?

EMMA: I don't know why he always has to put on a show

LILY: I don't know why she suddenly changed

CHRIS: I don't know why it feels like she can't always be herself

LILY: The thing is, in the end, it doesn't matter who you really are. What matters is what everyone else gets to see

CHRIS: Right?

EMMA: Right?

LILY: Right.

Scene 2

Instagram #1

LILY snaps a photo of herself wearing a new winter coat, sipping a coffee—it's autumn, leaves all around. A warm filter.

LILY: Nothing says back to school like new boots and my first pumpkin spice latte of the season. What do you say we spice things up this year? LOL let's have a great year! #backtoschool #newboots #coffee #yum #pumpkinspice #newbeginnings

Scene 3

Literally Dead

School hallway. LILY *waits, texting furiously.* EMMA *enters.*

EMMA: Hey!

LILY: Emma! Ohmigod, WHERE WERE YOU?

EMMA: The flight from Paris was seven hours, dude, I had to turn off my phone!

LILY: 'KAY, anyway, thank god you're home! I almost died.

EMMA: What? How?

LILY: I was so bored this summer I LITERALLY died, BUT anyway, WELCOME HOME—oh my god do you still speak English? *Parlais anglais? Voulez-vous coucher?*

EMMA: Oh my god stop.

LILY: Is that a baguette in your bag or are you just happy to see me?

EMMA: Oh how I missed you, Lily.

LILY: You missed me? GOOD. I missed you. But seriously, what happened? Look at your dress. Your shoes. I'm not worthy.

EMMA: The shopping was amazing. So was the program—

LILY: —yeah yeah you went to nerd school—

7

EMMA: —summer exchange program—

LILY: —but mostly I saw you posting epic Parisian selfies.

EMMA: I had a lot of fun.

LILY: So you like went out every night. Oh my god, emergency—did you make newer, cooler French friends?

EMMA: No, Lily, you're irreplaceable. I mean, mostly.

LILY: MOSTLY?!

EMMA: I'm kidding.

LILY: Oh my god you can't use your sophisticated French humor on us simple Canadians.

EMMA: Ha ha, fair enough.

LILY: Oh, WHAT ABOUT—

> *LILY scrolls through her phone, finds something, and thrusts it in EMMA's face.*

THIS?!

EMMA: Oh, right! Uh, one night there was this warehouse party—some guy from the program had a friend who works at a clothing store and he threw a huge rave all around the boxes of clothes and stuff.

LILY: Oh. My. God. That is the stuff of dreams! *Dreams*, I tell you!

EMMA: Such a good summer.

LILY: But like . . . you're glad to be back, right?

EMMA: Of course I am.

LILY: Okay, GOOD, whew. I was worried you were too cool for me now.

EMMA: Never!

LILY: Because, like, let's be real, this is some major makeover shit.

EMMA: What?!

LILY: Yeah, dude, no more baggy T-shirts! You're wearing ankle boots. Ankle boots!

EMMA: I wasn't that bad before.

LILY: It's more like one of those movies where the girl takes off her glasses—

EMMA: —and suddenly she's a babe, yes, yes, I'm familiar.

LILY: But I loved you all along. But, like, no summer romance. Seriously?

EMMA: Not really.

LILY: I didn't believe you at first when you told me that.

EMMA: Why wouldn't you believe me?

LILY: Because, A: I wondered if you were actually out banging dudes all summer but just too cool to confess the details of your amazing love affairs to me, but also, B: it seemed impossible that you could go to France and not meet some impossibly attractive poet named Jacques—

EMMA: Real creative.

LILY: —and sit under the shade of the Eiffel Tower writing lo-fi indie music together.

EMMA: You've really thought about this—

LILY: But then I also considered option c, that you remained captivatingly flirty yet distant, holding out hopes for a reunion with someone special back home . . .

EMMA: What are you talking about?

LILY: Nothing.

EMMA: Uh . . . anyway, how was your summer?

LILY: UM, well you already know because I texted you like every minute of my boring day. Being a lifeguard is the worst.

EMMA: You were texting while lifeguarding?

LILY: Well yeah until some lady complained.

EMMA: You are the worst!

LILY: What? I can watch people's dumb kids and text at the same time. I'm a multitasker.

EMMA: You haven't changed.

LILY: This is a momentous occasion. Let's take a pic!

EMMA: Reunited, and it feels so good!

LILY: I have taught you well.

> *LILY pulls EMMA in and snaps a selfie with her. EMMA awkwardly makes a silly face.*

Um, not our best—let's do another one:

EMMA: It's fine—

LILY: —no!

> *LILY takes another one—EMMA tries to smile for the camera, but she looks uncomfortable. LILY notices it but doesn't say anything.*

Uh—yeah! Cool. I'll throw some filters on that shit.

EMMA: Sweet. Uh, shouldn't we go to class?

LILY: I live on the edge.

EMMA: You're going to be late on the first day.

LILY: *Carpe diem,* bitch!

> *EMMA laughs and goes to leave.*

Wait, don't leave me!

EMMA: I am *literally* going to see you in five minutes.

LILY: Loveyoumissyoukbye!

EMMA: Kayloveyoubye!

EMMA leaves, passing CHRIS. As they walk by, they acknowledge each other—just a hair too late.

Hey, Chris.

CHRIS: What?

EMMA: I said, uh—hey!

CHRIS: Oh! Hey!

EMMA briefly considers saying something else, but leaves abruptly.

LILY: Brutal.

CHRIS: What?

LILY: Nothing. Hey, thanks for the ride, jerk.

CHRIS: Dude, you take forever to get ready. I'm not waiting for you just so you can make me take you to the Starbucks drive-through. Plus, Mom was all emotional.

LILY: Classic.

CHRIS: Dad spent like twenty minutes trying to take a picture with his iPad.

LILY: Ugh.

CHRIS: It's not even a big deal.

LILY: It IS a big deal. Grade Twelve is, like, the biggest of deals. And check THIS out:

LILY pulls the school-issued day planner out of her back-pack—it's got a big picture of CHRIS on the soccer field on the front page.

I'm basically seething with jealousy. Everyone in the entire school is going to forget to write their homework down on YOUR FACE.

CHRIS: Oh shit!

LILY: You're gonna have so many mustaches and dicks drawn on you.

CHRIS: Gimme that—

LILY: No! I want to deface it myself!

CHRIS: You're the worst.

LILY: Wait till Mom sees this: she's gonna WEEP.

CHRIS: Whatever. Anyway, Dad won tickets to the Bon Jovi concert tonight, so they're driving out to Aunt Lara's and staying the night.

LILY: Really?! Uhh, they're the worst.

CHRIS: Woah woah woah—Bon Jovi's *pretty* cool for an old dude.

LILY: You're the old dude here. Grade Twelve. You're basically dead.

CHRIS: Don't be a dick, Lil. Anyway, I'm in charge.

LILY: Ugh, whhyyy?!

CHRIS: Because I'm the favourite.

LILY: I would argue that, but I don't think I have a strong case.

CHRIS: I'm gonna have the team over tonight for some pizza and stuff, okay? It's just gonna be chill.

LILY: Well can I have some people over?

CHRIS: . . .

LILY: PLEASE, Chris, come on, I'm excited to see everyone and I was soooo lonely all summer except for my amazing, *beloved* big brother—

CHRIS: Hah. You're a monster.

LILY: I do mean it though. And this is your last year at school— we're NEVER GOING TO SEE YOU AGAIN.

CHRIS: That's not true. Come on, Lil, you know.

LILY: Don't even! This time next year you're already going to be doing keg stands with hot blond biology majors—

CHRIS: Okay, / that's enough—

LILY: / and hanging Bob Marley posters in your dorm room and you won't even remember your sister's NAME. You won't even remember you HAD a family.

CHRIS: Hey, just stop, okay?

LILY: Woah, sorry.

CHRIS: It's just a lot of pressure, y'know? I don't even know if I'll get into any programs or anything, so just chill out with the jokes.

LILY: Okay, okay. I didn't realize you were having a life crisis about it.

CHRIS: I'm not—just—whatever.

LILY: No, I get it. Grad is kind of terrifying. You're going from a school where everyone knows and is unreasonably obsessed with you, to a place where you are one of thousands, basically insignificant and unknown.

CHRIS: Wow, thanks for putting it that way.

LILY: Well, I'm just laughing so I don't literally cry. I'm going to miss you next year.

CHRIS: Really?

LILY: Yeah, yeah, don't rub it in. But yes, I will. So we have to make this year memorable. That's all I'm saying.

CHRIS: Yeah.

LILY: So it's cool if you don't want to start the year off in deep shit with our parents. We'll be respectful tonight.

CHRIS: No.

LILY: No?

CHRIS: I have an idea.

Scene 4

Instagram #2 / Endless Summer

LILY snaps a picture: LILY with a trendy alcoholic drink in a low-cut top and tons of makeup, maybe CHRIS wearing sunglasses in a tight T-shirt and holding a beer. As it appears on screen she reads the caption:

LILY: HOUSE PARTY!! #tanktops #shortskirts #endlesssummer #getleiid #likehawaiigetit?

(to audience) Yeah, okay, it's raining and like ten degrees out, but who doesn't love a Hawaiian themed party?! Before we know it—

Her phone beeps and vibrates. LILY and CHRIS read the comments to the audience.

Yaaaaaaas

CHRIS: Can I bring some friends?

LILY: whats ur address

CHRIS: omg I'm gonna wear a bikini

LILY: im bringin a pineapple!

CHRIS: imma puke in yer bathtub

LILY: best first day of school ever!!!!!

Lights rise on EMMA and LILY in LILY's room.

EMMA: Can't I just do what I always do? I just want to spend the party eating chips and making bitchy comments about people's poor behaviour.

LILY: Don't be a bummer, dude. You need a drink.

EMMA: Don't be such a pusher! You're the kind of person the counsellors warned us about.

LILY: Yeah, my friendship is a total gateway drug.

CHRIS shouts through the door:

CHRIS: Do we need more ice?

LILY: *(shouting back)* Go look in the bathtub, idiot, it's literally full—we're fine!

EMMA: Okay, *WHAT* is happening with my hair right now? Why is this not working? Ugh, screw it.

LILY: Look, I know maybe you're bummed about being home—

EMMA: —I'm not—

LILY: But I just want us to have fun tonight.

EMMA: I know. I'm just feeling—I don't know. Weird. Maybe it's jet lag.

LILY: Okay, real talk. Can I ask you a question?

EMMA: I'm probably going to hate this, aren't I?

LILY: Ya, maybe. So. Do you *like* Chris?

EMMA: Uh—

LILY: And I guess before you answer I just want to tell you that A: I already know and B: It's totally okay.

EMMA: What does that leave me to answer?

LILY: Just tell me the truth.

EMMA: Well . . . I don't know.

LILY: It's okay, dude—

EMMA: Kind of.

LILY: Kind of?

EMMA: Yeah, I guess. Since that time I went up to the cottage with you guys.

LILY: That was like a million years ago.

EMMA: If by a million years you mean Grade Nine, then yeah.

LILY: Why didn't you say anything?

EMMA: Come on.

LILY: No, why?

EMMA: Well, first of all, he's your brother and I didn't want to be creepy.

LILY: Oh my god, not creepy—I would much rather it be you than the usual skanks who're into him. There are things written about him on the bathroom walls of our school that I can never unsee.

EMMA: Exactly though—that's the thing. He's like, *Chris*. I just can't ever really see him being into someone like me.

LILY: Yeah, the like "school" version of Chris. But actual Chris and actual Emma . . . well, you actually *know* him.

EMMA: At school he's like a different person.

LILY: Yeah, I know. I mean, like, those girls he dates? He never sticks with them because he can't keep up that act. They think he's this super bro, but / he's not.

CHRIS shouts through the door.

CHRIS: I think we need chips!

LILY: *(shouting back)* THEN GO BUY SOME CHIPS, YOU LOSER!

(to EMMA) See? But once people get here he's gonna be all like, "Hey, bruhhhhhh," and people will think he is cool, which he is NOT.

EMMA: Right, but I guess what I'm trying to say is, no one thinks *I'm* cool—people at school mostly only know me as "Lily's friend." I think everyone still sees me as the, like, chunky awkward girl from Grade Six, and I kind of think he does too.

LILY: Well, I happen to know for a fact that that's not true. But anyway, like—when I saw those pics of you in Paris, I was like, *yes.* That's my girl. That's my amazing, talented, smart, beautiful friend. I've known you were amazing all along, and now I feel like you're starting to figure it out too. Now it's time to let everyone see what I see. You've had your, like, glasses off, hair-out-of-the-bun moment, now you just gotta make your entrance where everyone's like, "WoooAAAAHHH, who's that?!"

EMMA: Thank you, Lily.

LILY: You're welcome. Now I demand you shut up and take a shot *immediately.*

They take a shot and chase it with sips of their drinks.

EMMA: Okay. I'm doing this. I'm doing this!

LILY: That's my girl. Now don't come out of this room until you look like a Kardashian.

LILY leaves. Through the next section, EMMA puts on more makeup. She takes a selfie. It appears on the screen behind her briefly, and she turns to look at it before deleting it. Loud music plays. CHRIS and LILY talk.

CHRIS: You're kidding me.

LILY: Holy shit.

CHRIS: Lil, how many people did you invite?

LILY: Only my Insta followers!

CHRIS: Dude, that's like thousands of people.

LILY: Okay, HALF of those people are middle-aged creepers I don't know. But yeah the other half is basically the whole school.

CHRIS: Jesus.

LILY: Ye shall live forever in legend.

CHRIS: Hopefully for the right reasons.

LILY: *(to the audience)* It's amazing

CHRIS: Fifty of Lily's girlfriends have showed up wearing sundresses

LILY: We put on sunscreen so we smell like the beach

CHRIS: And then Tyler brings out a forty of vodka

LILY: Shot!

CHRIS: And off we go

LILY: Woo!

CHRIS: *(to LILY)* If we get busted it's all on you, okay?

LILY: No way, if the po' come I'm sending them right to you. Because you're the *favourite*, right?

CHRIS: You're the worst.

LILY: Emma's missing it!

CHRIS: Why is it so hot?

LILY: *(to audience)* I turn up the heat so it feels like it's still hot outside

EMMA: *(to audience)* I open the door and it's a wall of heat and noise and bare skin

LILY: Ohmigod, EMMA!

CHRIS: *(to audience)* There's gotta be a hundred people here now

LILY: You're a freakin' BABE. Now take a shot with me.

EMMA: I think I'm good for now—

LILY: Are we doing this, or are we doing this?

> *EMMA considers for a moment, and then they take the shot.*
> *LILY turns to CHRIS.*

Chris, it's a party. Parties are fun. There are a billion people here. It's gonna be awesome. People will still like you even if we run out of ice.

CHRIS: You're the worst.

LILY: And yet also the best!

CHRIS: Let's do this.

> *He takes a shot.*

Yeeah!

EMMA: *(to audience)* And there he is

LILY: *(to audience)* "Party Chris"

CHRIS: Yo, Damien!

EMMA: *(to audience)* I can tell he's worried about impressing people, but no matter how he's feeling, Chris can always put on a smile

LILY: *(to audience)* And suddenly he's hosting this party

CHRIS: Turn it up!

LILY: *(to audience)* See?

CHRIS: What's up, bruuuuuuh?

LILY: SHUTUPSHUTUP, Maya is actually wearing a bikini

EMMA: *(to audience)* It's amazing

LILY: YAAAAAS

> LILY *takes a picture of the two of them. The music gets louder.*

EMMA: *(to audience)* The guys from Chris's team are loving it

LILY: OH MY GOD, I LOVE THIS SONG

EMMA: *(to audience)* The girls are dancing in the living room. Every window in the house is fogged up

LILY: *(to audience)* I'm sweating

CHRIS: *(to audience)* They're sweating

EMMA: *(to audience)* Everybody's sweating

LILY: I LOVE IT

EMMA: *(to audience)* I go to the kitchen

CHRIS: Ha ha, somebody actually brought a pineapple!

LILY: *(to audience)* Emma looks SUPER hot

EMMA: *(to audience)* Lily is already wasted

LILY: Look at your hair!

EMMA: *(to audience)* But every guy is looking at her

CHRIS: Gross, guys, cut that shit out!

LILY: Shot!

EMMA: *(to audience)* And I think—I'm here. He's here. This time things are going to be different

CHRIS: Hey, Emma.

EMMA: It's uh, so . . . hot.

CHRIS: Yeah it's . . . hot.

Awkward beat.

LILY: Wowkgottagobye!

Blackout. The music stops.

EMMA: *(to audience)* And all of a sudden

LILY: I hit the lights.

(to party) SHHH!

EMMA: *(to audience)* Everyone is quiet

CHRIS: Is someone at the door?

LILY: *(to audience)* There's no one at the door

EMMA: *(to audience)* Chris is beside me

CHRIS: *(to audience)* Emma is right beside me

EMMA: *(to audience)* My arm brushes his

CHRIS: *(to audience)* She's right there

EMMA: *(to audience)* And he just grabs my hand

CHRIS: *(to audience)* It's dark, and everyone is quiet

EMMA: *(to audience)* Girls are giggling

CHRIS: *(to audience)* And we're just here

EMMA: *(to audience)* Together

CHRIS: *(to EMMA)* Hey

EMMA: *(to CHRIS)* Oh hey

CHRIS: *(to EMMA)* Having fun?

LILY: *(to audience)* And then they kiss?

CHRIS leans in to EMMA, but she awkwardly blurts:

EMMA: *(to CHRIS)* Are you having fun?

CHRIS: *(to EMMA)* I just asked you that.

EMMA: *(to CHRIS)* Sorry.

LILY: *(to audience)* Dammit, Emma.

(to party) FALSE ALARM. Shut the windows, bitches!

> *The music starts again, louder than before. Pictures flash on the screen behind them, blurrier and more random than before.*

CHRIS: *(to audience)* The party starts again

EMMA: *(to audience)* It gets hotter and hotter

CHRIS: *(to audience)* The guys are taking off their shirts

LILY: SELFIE!

> *LILY pulls CHRIS and EMMA in for a selfie.*

CHRIS: *(to audience)* I've never seen everyone this drunk before

EMMA: *(to audience)* I can't talk to him

CHRIS: *(to audience)* I don't think I've been this drunk /
before, but—

LILY: / SHOTS!

EMMA, LILY, and CHRIS do shots.

EMMA: Ugh, I need water.

CHRIS: *(to audience)* I should probably lock my parents' bed-room—naaaasty, there's already someone in there

LILY: OMIGOD, YOU'RE KIDDING ME.

CHRIS: *(to audience)* It's getting intense in here

EMMA: *(to audience)* I stumble to the bathroom to catch my breath

LILY: EMMA.

EMMA enters the bathroom and the music and shouting grow quiet. EMMA takes a breath. The pictures on the screen become blurrier.

Emma: I'M COMING IN.

EMMA: Wait, I'm—

LILY: I need to pee.

LILY enters the washroom.

What's wrong?

EMMA: Just give me a second, okay, I feel like I'm gonna puke—

LILY: NOPE, NOPE. You're weening out.

EMMA: No, I'm not. It's just—I don't even know how to describe it, it's like I try to say things and I just choke and I'm just saying stupid nothing words like an idiot and I wonder if it's better if I don't even try. I just wanna go home—

LILY: Stop! I know what you're trying to do, and I don't want to hear you say that. Okay? That's enough. Because you are talking about my favourite person in the whole world.

EMMA: You?

LILY: No, you bitch, I'm talking about you. It makes me sad to hear you say that. It makes me *sad* to hear you say that, okay? I love you.

EMMA: I love you too, / Lily.

LILY: Like—okay, I just—I'm really nervous, okay? Like I don't want anything to change between us because you like went to Paris and found yourself and shit, and I just wanted to throw you this big-ass amazing party so you don't forget 'bout me—

EMMA: Lily, I'd never forget about you.

LILY: I just saw these pics of you at the Eiffel Tower and stuff and I was like, wow, we're growing up and shit is changing and maybe we're not going to be friends forever and I like freaked the fuck out, you know? 'Cause, like, you're my *person*. I don't want to be creepy and I don't even know why I'm so—

EMMA: You're my person too, Lily. You don't need to be worried. I'm not going anywhere. I'm just figuring myself out right now.

LILY: I know. I know. OKAY, REAL TALK, shake it off. Come here. Look. Your hair is large and amazing, your boobs look awesom-mmmeeee in that dress, and you smell like a fancy drink from Milestones. You are amazing. And I'm not the only one who thinks so. Go talk to Chris, okay? Tonight is the night. You're the two best people I know, and you're running out of time because he's gonna go away, and—okay I am like totally not crying in the bathroom because that's like literally a cliché. But go get what you deserve.

LILY opens the door.

You know what to do.

LILY leaves the bathroom. EMMA stands, staring at her-self in the mirror. CHRIS stands, looking at himself in the mirror in his room. The party sounds remain muffled from the other side of the door. They take a breath, and then move. Simultaneously, CHRIS and EMMA open their doors, facing each other in the hallway.

EMMA: *(to CHRIS)* Hi.

CHRIS: *(to EMMA)* Hi—are you all right?

EMMA: Yeah, it's just super hot out there, and the first day back and everything and—

CHRIS: It's a lot, yeah. I know the feeling.

They share a smile.

EMMA: Did Lily say something to you?

CHRIS: She said about a billion things, most of which were "yaaaas."

They laugh.

EMMA: Never mind.

CHRIS: No, what?

EMMA: Nothing!

CHRIS: What is it what is it?

EMMA laughs.

EMMA: Nothing!!

CHRIS: Do you have something to tell me?

EMMA: Oh—I just thought, because you grabbed my hand—

CHRIS: Emma.

He kisses her.

EMMA: Oh!

CHRIS: Emma. Uhhh, I uh—I just. Um. Yeah, I uhhh—

This goes on for a while.

EMMA: I just—

CHRIS: Wait, hang on, I'm just trying to— I'm not very— Uh. Okay, I'm gonna use a metaphor. Like you know that picture on the stupid—uh thing?

EMMA: The school agenda?

CHRIS: Yeah. That picture, I know it looks like cool and stuff but I totally remember what I was thinking during that game. When I was in juniors our coach from the seniors team would always like joke around and stuff, and when we were leaving the locker room he'd slap us on the back and say, "Don't fuck up!" And like—he was kidding—but no one wanted to be the guy who fucked up, you know? And I guess that kinda stayed with me. Okay, I know this doesn't make any sense yet but I promise I have a, uh, point—um. So yeah, I think about that every time I step on the field. It's this huge thing now. And that's what I was thinking when that picture was taken—it was our last chance to take it home, and I had the ball. I was, like, looking up at the goal post, and then lining up my shot. But like—I don't think they'd want to use the photo if everyone knew what I was thinking. Not exactly inspiring. Don't fuck up. Don't fuck up.

And, like, I guess the thing is that I was scared to ever say anything to you about how I feel 'cause, like, I don't want to fuck it up. You're special, and like—I'm not. I'm so not. No one knows that but I think you do so I guess I just didn't think you'd ever like me, because you know the truth. Does that make any sense?

EMMA: I like you.

CHRIS: Cool.

He smiles.

Cool.

EMMA: Do you wanna dance?

CHRIS: Like right here in the hallway?

EMMA: Mmmmyeah.

CHRIS: Okay then.

He smiles.

They dance awkwardly, their arms around each other.

(*to audience*) I'm not a great dancer

EMMA: (*to audience*) He's hanging on tight

CHRIS: (*to audience*) I'm doing my best

EMMA: (*to audience*) He smells so good

CHRIS: (*to audience*) She smells like the beach

EMMA: (*to audience*) I can really feel that last shot kicking in

CHRIS: (*to audience*) She's holding on to me

EMMA: (*to audience*) He has nice arms

CHRIS: (*to audience*) She's got her eyes closed

EMMA: (*to audience*) The room is spinning so I lean my head against his shoulder

CHRIS: (*to audience*) It's really happening

EMMA: (*to audience*) I like this

CHRIS: Are you having fun?

EMMA: This is fun.

CHRIS: Yeah?

EMMA: This is the best.

CHRIS: You're the best.

> *She pulls him in and they kiss.* LILY *enters and silently reacts ecstatically. She stifles a laugh as she snaps a pic of them, then a selfie with them in the background, and then creeps away, unnoticed.*

Wanna go somewhere quieter?

> EMMA *smiles.*

(to audience) I grab her hand, we go to my room. I close the door.

LILY: TURN IT UP!

> *The music swells, pictures flash on the screens, reaching a crescendo and then cutting out abruptly.*

Scene 5

Instagram #3

> *The trashed living room at* LILY *and* CHRIS's *house. A bikini hangs from a lamp.*

LILY: Y'all are ANIMALS. Party animals amirite?! #morningafter #hangover #mcdonalds #mayhavejustpuked #twice

Scene 6

Aftermath

EMMA: It's five a.m. and I'm walking down the street. I have my things. I feel awful. My hands are shaking. I feel like maybe I'm still drunk, but the air is cold and I just want to get home. Suddenly my knees buckle and I'm sitting on the pavement. Blurry whiteness closes in on my vision, and before I know it I'm throwing up on the sidewalk by the bus stop, heave after heave of vodka and pineapple juice and tequila and Smirnoff ice and eyeliner and sunscreen and sweat on the sidewalk for everyone to see. Just breathe, I think. Just breathe.

Scene 7

Legendary

CHRIS: Holy shit.

First thing I did was drag myself to the kitchen and make some coffee. Put on some tunes and just start cleaning up—there's like a million beer cans on every table and chair and obviously a ton on the floor. There was someone's T-shirt in the freezer and a phone in the kitchen sink. Awesome. It was the best night ever. Legendary. Everyone had the best time, and Lily and I are party gods. But that's not even the best part.

The best part was Emma.

Scene 8

Details

Lunchtime, outside.

LILY: OMIGOD, what a party. Like, legendary enough to make even YOU late for school. Amazing.

Beat.

I like, crawled to McDonald's and then got all the coconut water I could carry and it was basically a miracle cure 'cause I feel like *totally fine.* P.S., there was *no one* here this morning. It was hilarious. English class was ONLY the randoms and people who don't have Instagram. Like it was noticeable. By the way, Instagram was *amazing* today, some pretty epic party pics—haha I got a few good ones of you, but don't worry, I didn't post them. *Omigod* this reminds me, Chris told me that Tyson actually puked in his shoes and then WORE THEM HOME. What a guy. Amazing. I mean, did you not have the best time?

Beat.

Are you mad at me?

EMMA: What?

LILY: You didn't text me back this morning and like—oh my god, you are. Whatever I did, I am *so sorry.*

EMMA: No—

LILY: Oh my god, okay GOOD, because I totally don't hold myself responsible for anything I did under the influence of tequila!

Pause.

Okay, dude, you're KILLING ME. How did it go last night with Chris? You guys are . . . a thing?

EMMA: I think so.

LILY: What do you mean?

EMMA: I uh. Yeah. Yes!

LILY: Omigod YES. Amazing.

EMMA: But like . . . I haven't talked to him since—

LILY: Umm, then talk to him, you weirdo.

EMMA: I just—uh.

LILY: What?

EMMA: I don't remember.

EMMA laughs.

LILY: . . .

EMMA: Like I don't really remember anything.

LILY: Oh my god! That's hilarious. You guys fully, fully made out.

EMMA: Oh my god.

LILY: Yeah, it was kind of gross to watch but cute in theory.

Beat.

EMMA: I don't remember that. At all.

LILY: Dude, you had like thirty shots, obviously you're going to black out for some of it.

EMMA: Right.

LILY: What *do* you remember?

EMMA: Uh, like people dancing, tequila. Your weepy pep talk in the bathroom—

LILY: *(hands over ears)* Lalalala, you're not reminding me of anything embarrassing!

EMMA: And then I guess—talking to Chris? I think?

LILY: Well there ya go. Just text him, dude! You're allowed to do that now, you know. That's kind of how it works. Now that you're a thaaaaang.

EMMA: Yeah, I will. I totally will.

LILY: And you're not gonna wimp out?

EMMA: No. Of course not.

LILY: Cool.

Beat.

Oh my god, did I tell you Maya texted me looking for her bikini?

Scene 9

Hey

CHRIS texts EMMA. On the other side of the stage, EMMA receives his texts but doesn't know how to respond.

CHRIS: hey

didn't see you at school this morning! I was so hungover I almost didn't go.

I found that pineapple under the couch, haha

The next day:

I had a really amazing time at the party, I hope you did too

I was so happy yesterday.

Later that night:

Hey maybe you've been busy, but wanna get dinner tonight?

Beat.

You there?

Scene 10

I Love Paris

EMMA *speaks to the audience.*

EMMA: I look at this one picture I took in Paris almost every day. It's the night of the warehouse party, and I'm all dressed up. I had finally figured out how to put on fake eyelashes, and I'm wearing this beautiful shirt I got at the Montaigne Market. It's dark out and there's no flash, but my face is lit up just by all the shimmering lights of the city. My hair is blowing softly in the wind, and the picture is blurry, just a bit, because I was walking when I took it.

I look at it every day because I think I'm looking for something. I'm looking for something I can't see anymore. Something that was there, just for a moment. Or maybe not.

I don't know.

Scene 11

Tritext

EMMA, CHRIS, *and* LILY *are texting.*

LILY: (*to* EMMA) sup gurl

EMMA: (*to* LILY) Not much, you?

LILY: (*to* EMMA) straight up not doing homework

EMMA: *(to LILY)* nice

LILY: *(to EMMA)* sup for you tonight

EMMA: *(to LILY)* Probably straight-up doing homework.

LILY: *(to EMMA)* so is there a reason your avoiding chris?

EMMA: *(to LILY)* What do you mean?

LILY: *(to EMMA)* its been like 2 days since the party and you won't talk to him

EMMA: *(to LILY)* I've been busy

LILY: *(to EMMA)* dude I literally see you every day I know you're not busy

EMMA: *(to LILY)* Fair.

CHRIS: *(to LILY)* yo

EMMA: *(to LILY)* Can I ask you something?

LILY: *(to EMMA)* hang on Chris is texting me

(to CHRIS) what do you want old man

EMMA: *(to LILY)* k

CHRIS: *(to LILY)* you're a douche

LILY: *(to CHRIS)* get off my lawn!

CHRIS: *(to LILY)* you're satan. anyway have you talked to Emma?

LILY: *(to EMMA)* hes asking about you! like he has every day since the party!

CHRIS: *(to LILY)* I just want to know whats up

LILY: *(to EMMA)* what do I saaaayyyy

CHRIS: *(to LILY)* did she say anything to you?

LILY: *(to EMMA)* no response, okay thanks Emma real helpful!!!!

(to CHRIS) nope, nothing

CHRIS: *(to LILY)* k I gtg back to practice, lemme know what I should do

LILY: *(to EMMA)* okay seriously what is up?

EMMA: *(to LILY)* Can we just talk like . . . face to face?

LILY: *(to EMMA)* Yes, of course.

>   LILY *facetimes* EMMA—*they're in their respective bedrooms.*

What's going on?

EMMA: Ugh, I don't know. I guess I'm just not good at guy stuff.

LILY: Guys are not that complicated.

EMMA: Well, not for you.

LILY: Hey, thanks!

EMMA: No, I didn't mean it like that, I'm just—ugh I don't know, I'm just being a weirdo.

LILY: Well what's the problem? Are you just shy about hanging out?

EMMA: I guess so. I mean, we haven't ever just hung out one on one before.

LILY: Except at the party.

EMMA: Right. You said Chris and I disappeared for a while . . .

LILY: Ya, you sure did.

EMMA: Right.

LILY: Shit, dude, you don't remember that either?

EMMA: I was nervous so I kept doing shots. It was dumb.

LILY: Didn't you learn to hold your liquor in Paris?

EMMA: Apparently not.

LILY: But are you just going to avoid Chris forever now?

EMMA: No—

LILY: 'Cause I have had to watch you guys staring lovingly at each other for like two years now, so I don't really want to go back to that.

EMMA: Of course not.

LILY: Then what's the problem?

EMMA: I've just been kind of freaking out because I'm not on birth control or anything—

LILY: Oh my god. THAT'S why you've been so weird.

EMMA: / Well, yeah, and—

LILY: Oh my god, my excitement over you finally popping your cherry / is only dampened by being kind of weirded out that you had sex with my brother.

EMMA: That is the grossest phrase you could possibly use.

LILY: But anyway, Emma, it's okay! It's always terrible the first time. And it hurts and shit like that. But if you're worried about pregnancy or whatever, just go see your doctor.

EMMA: Yeah?

LILY: It's not a big deal at all. I'm sorry you were so worried about it. I wish you'd just said something before! Do you want me to go with you to the doctor?

EMMA: No, it's okay.

LILY: So are you gonna be normal with Chris now?

EMMA: Sure.

LILY: I mean you don't have to, it's just—I thought you guys were really into each other.

EMMA: I am, like a lot—you know that.

LILY: Well, good. I'm sorry that it wasn't awesome the first time, but it almost never is. Maybe now you can move past it?

EMMA: Totally. I want to move past it.

LILY: OKAY, so since we are both straight up not doing homework now, why don't you call your doctor and make an appointment. THEN once the ice is broken, you and Chris can do the texting because I already kind of feel like your mom right now and I'm defs not arranging a booty call for you.

EMMA: Hah, sure. Thanks, Lily.

LILY: Of course. You know you can tell me anything, right?

EMMA: Of course.

LILY: Love you, girl.

EMMA: Love you too.

LILY: Kbye.

EMMA: Kbye!

> LILY *hangs up and immediately begins texting.* EMMA *sits, staring ahead.*

Scene 12

Instagram #4

A selfie of LILY, CHRIS, and EMMA from halfway through the party—they look great but very drunk.

LILY: #TBT earlier this week (lol) The nights you'll never remember with the people you'll never forget. Thanks everyone for a great party—the year is off to an amazing start!

Scene 13

Hanging Out

LILY, CHRIS, and EMMA are hanging out at school. CHRIS and EMMA sit side by side.

LILY: Okay so, like, I *know* I'm only in Grade Eleven, but I was *volunteering* my services for the prom and they said NO! I cannot believe it. I can't.

EMMA: Dude, I can. Why would they have someone on the committee that's not in the grad class?

CHRIS: Actually, why would you even want to be on the committee?

LILY: So I can get a practice run for my prom, duh.

CHRIS: Yeah for a second I thought you just wanted to help.

EMMA: How naive, Christopher.

LILY: Oh my god no, you are not allowed to gang up on me together now.

CHRIS: Too laaa-aaaate!

LILY: Ugh no, I'm supposed to be both of your favourite person at the same time and it's supposed to be great.

CHRIS: It's all your fault, Lil. Just think, I only have my G2, so I can only drive one person. Guess who I'm gonna pick?

LILY: This is a literal nightmare.

EMMA: I just want to clarify—you do know what "literal" actually means right?

LILY: I figuratively do not care.

CHRIS: Yeah, she's smarter than she looks.

LILY: I hate you both. I'm going to give the world's most embarrassing speech about both of you at your wedding.

An awkward silence.

Okay, awkward. Too soon?

CHRIS: Sorry, I'm just super tired. I had early practice this morning.

EMMA: I've got a chem exam I should study for. I'mma go.

LILY: Okay, bye! I'll turn away so you can make out!

She turns away.

CHRIS: Happy studying. Want to meet up later?

EMMA: Sure. Uh—bye.

He wants to kiss her but she grabs her bag off the ground. He gently stops her, and mouths "you okay?" so LILY can't hear. EMMA smiles and says "yeah" and kisses him on the cheek. CHRIS watches her as she goes. LILY turns back, eyes covered, and gives CHRIS a thumbs up.

LILY: Nice.

Beat.

Oh my god I'm still totally mad about prom!

Scene 14

Countdown

EMMA addresses the audience.

EMMA: It's been sixty-eight hours since the party. I've had thirteen hours of sleep since then

It's one hour till my doctor's appointment

I have a million questions to ask

Fourteen blocks to my doctor's office

Fifty-nine minutes left

Breathe. Just breathe

Scene 15

Flowers

Later that night, outside.

EMMA: Hi.

CHRIS: Hey, what's up.

EMMA: Not much.

CHRIS: You look pretty.

EMMA: Oh—

CHRIS: Ha ha, what?

EMMA: Oh no, I mean—uh thank you. Thanks.

CHRIS: Of course.

EMMA: Wow, I'm not good at this whole "accepting compliments" thing, am I?

CHRIS: I think you're great at it.

EMMA: What?

CHRIS: That was a test . . . a compliment?

EMMA: OH ha ha. Right. Yes. Well I fail.

Pause. CHRIS smiles at her.

CHRIS: I was glad you wanted to see me. I wanted to see you—you know, just us.

EMMA: Really?

CHRIS: Well it's hard to have a conversation when Lily is around.

EMMA: Haha right.

CHRIS: I just feel like things have been weird, and I was kind of worried I did something wrong—I mean, like, I always kinda feel like I'm gonna screw things up and maybe I put too much pressure on things, but I just wanted to make it up to you so I uh—

He pulls a crushed bouquet of cheap flowers from his bag.

Ah shit.

She laughs.

They looked really nice before. I just wanted them to be a surprise, but I guess they got squished.

EMMA: It's okay, they're beautiful, thank you.

CHRIS: Cool.

She laughs again.

Uh, is that a "laughing with me" or "laughing at me." I can't tell.

EMMA: I'm just laughing.

CHRIS: Okay, cool.

EMMA: Thank you.

She takes the flowers and holds them.

CHRIS: I hope you have a vase or something at home.

EMMA: I do.

CHRIS: They're kinda wilted.

EMMA: You can cut a bit of the stems off. That way they get more water.

CHRIS: Ha see, that's the kind of stuff I don't know. You always know those things.

EMMA: This is so weird.

CHRIS: Oh. Like . . . good weird?

EMMA: Good weird.

CHRIS: Good.

A moment. EMMA puts the bouquet down. CHRIS leans in to kiss EMMA. They kiss for a second and then she pulls away.

Oh—I'm sorry.

EMMA: No, no it's fine.

CHRIS: I thought we were—

EMMA: No, it's okay.

She kisses him. When they part, she looks at him.

(suddenly) I have to ask you something.

CHRIS: Sure.

EMMA: Okay. Okay. Umm. What happened at the party?

CHRIS: We . . . well we danced, and we—what do you mean?

EMMA: I don't remember.

CHRIS: Okay.

Pause.

You don't remember? I-uh-uh. Okay.

EMMA: What?

CHRIS: Because. I said something that I had like really wanted to say for a long time, and I—oh shit. Okay.

EMMA: Oh.

CHRIS: Well I feel stupid now.

EMMA: Don't feel stupid.

CHRIS: Okay, I guess I'll just have to tell you again.

EMMA: Just—stop for a second

CHRIS: What's wrong?

EMMA: I just—okay. Okay. I went to see my doctor because I wanted to—I just didn't know if you used—

CHRIS: I did, of course I did—

EMMA: —just don't—don't talk right now, okay? She just kept asking me questions, and I couldn't really answer, and I think I said something . . . I don't know. But she sent me to the hospital for an exam and they called the police—

CHRIS: Why would they do that?

EMMA: I don't know. They think someone hurt me.

CHRIS: Hurt you like how?

Beat.

EMMA: I don't *remember*—do you understand?

CHRIS: No no, I don't understand.

EMMA: I mean, I can tell that we . . . but I . . .

She gathers herself.

I wanted to tell you that they're going to call your parents.

CHRIS: Why?

EMMA: Because of the party. I just said—I don't know, I just said that I couldn't remember what happened but that it was at the party—

CHRIS: Oh my god.

EMMA: It's okay, it's gonna be okay, it's just that I just—I guess I had too much to drink and I don't remember—

CHRIS: So they think I—?

EMMA: No, no, I didn't say anything about us. I'm so sorry, and I just wanted to warn you because I didn't want to get anyone involved. I didn't mean to make this whole thing happen—

CHRIS: Are you going to say something about . . . about— that we—

EMMA: No, I won't tell them. Of course not. I won't.

Beat. EMMA's phone beeps. She immediately looks at it.

It's my mom, she's picking me up. I have to go. Right now.

CHRIS: Wait—

He hands her the flowers.

EMMA: I can't take those home, okay? I'm sorry.

She exits quickly. CHRIS sits, holding the flowers.

Scene 16

Instagram #5 / Comment Storm

A picture of a cop car through a living-room window.

LILY: guess you can party too hard lol #nofuncity #partylegends #Ilovemeninuniform

LILY, CHRIS, and EMMA read the comments to the audience.

EMMA: Lol epic

LILY: booooo

CHRIS: see you in jail party people

LILY: omg save us from underage drinking

CHRIS: haha

EMMA: amazing

LILY: legendary!!

Scene 17

Family

LILY and CHRIS at home.

CHRIS: Why would you post a picture of that? Delete it.

LILY: Whatever. This is some bullshit. If the police knew about the party, why didn't they come on the night?

CHRIS: I don't know.

LILY: What did they ask you? / I mean, they asked me if people were drinking and I said I didn't know.

CHRIS: They—

LILY: I mean, they can't prove it anyway, right? Like if they're not there to catch it in person, right?

CHRIS: I don't know.

LILY: Like if there was a noise complaint, they're supposed to come check it out so they can't get mad now. Ugh.

CHRIS: Did you tell Emma they came here?

LILY holds up her phone.

LILY: I already posted the pic. Everyone knows already, dude. Chill out.

CHRIS: I just—I would never hurt her. Never. You know that.

LILY: *Hurt* her? What the fuck, Chris? What are you talking about?

CHRIS: Didn't she tell you?

Beat.

She went to the doctor / and they . . . uh—

LILY: / Yeah . . . what?

CHRIS: They called the police. They said that . . . something . . . something bad happened at the party. That's why they came here.

Long pause.

Anyway, she didn't say anything about her and me.

LILY: Oh my god.

CHRIS: I know.

LILY: No it's just . . . oh shit, Emma.

CHRIS: I don't know. I don't know what to do. I mean, what if they arrest me, or-or—

LILY: It's fine. It's going to be fine. Listen, it's just a misunderstanding. She was asking me about pregnancy and stuff and I told her to just get checked out if she was worried.

CHRIS: Oh.

LILY: She's just nervous because it was her first time.

CHRIS: What?

LILY: You didn't do anything wrong. / And whatever, you guys hooked up—

CHRIS: / Of course not—

LILY: —and Emma just freaked out / and the doctor totally overreacted.

CHRIS: / I just don't know why she—

LILY: And no one saw you guys / together—

CHRIS: / Are you sure?

LILY: And even if they did, they can't prove anything or like—

CHRIS: / Prove what?

LILY: —say that you did anything bad—

CHRIS pulls his hood over his head and covers his face.

—so we don't need to freak out. Chris? Like you're doing right now? Uh, can you, like, not do that right now?

CHRIS: Can you, like, let me talk for a second? How about that?

Beat.

LILY: Yeah. Whatever. Sorry. Yeah.

CHRIS pulls his hood back down. He takes a deep breath.

Okay. What did she say to you?

CHRIS: They don't know we hooked up. They think it was someone else and that it was something bad.

LILY: Okay. Well that's fine. I know Emma, she's not going to say anything. No one saw you together at the party, and even if they tried to blame you, everyone knows you're a good guy and it's not going to stick because nothing bad happened. Right?

CHRIS: Right. Do you believe me?

LILY: Of course I believe you. I'll talk to Emma. It's gonna be fine.

    LILY hugs CHRIS.

CHRIS: Just—just delete that photo of the cop car, okay?

LILY: I'm *not* going to delete that photo. Because we have nothing to hide. It's okay, Chris. I promise. But like . . .

CHRIS: What?

LILY: Maybe don't let people see you talking to Emma.

Scene 18

Questions

CHRIS talks to a group of his friends, putting on a show.

CHRIS: Dude, it was nuts—so this cop, huge guy, comes and knocks on the door. And I'm like, "Oh fuck, what am I gonna say," and I'm like trying to make a choice about what's believable, right?

So he says, "Was there a party here on Tuesday night?" and I'm like, "Yes, sir," and he said, "Was there any alcohol involved?" and I'm like, "No, sir, we're all in high school," and the whole time I'm thinking, "Shit, I hope the recycling is gone, or we're fucked!"

And I know he doesn't believe me, but what is he gonna say, right? And so I just keep fuckin' smiling and saying "yes, sir" and "no, sir" and "I don't know, sir" until he goes. I was sweating though, dude.

I don't know why they're interviewing more people at school though, that's so weird . . . Emma? Yeah, I kind of know her. She's my sister's friend.

The cop said what?

Why would they think that?

That's so stupid. I don't know anything about that. Whatever.

Scene 19

Comment Storm #2

EMMA, CHRIS, and LILY read the comments.

EMMA: Um

CHRIS: Um

LILY: Um

EMMA / CHRIS / LILY: Okay

LILY: what's with the freaky interviews

EMMA: oh my god did something like terrible happen and none of us knew?!

CHRIS: I puked in my shoes, that was pretty bad

LILY: no like actually though

EMMA: 'cause that would be fucked up

CHRIS: the cop kept asking me about like girls and stuff

LILY: what do you mean?

EMMA: yeah what r u talking about

CHRIS: like if anything weird was going on with guys and girls . . .

LILY: woah

EMMA: oh my GOD that's fucked up

CHRIS: well, I saw a girl talking to the police . . .

LILY: me too

EMMA: who?!

CHRIS: uhh I'll text you about it

LILY: that's terrible

EMMA: does that mean there's like, someone out there?

CHRIS: shit

LILY: that's scary, I hope they find him

CHRIS: me too

EMMA: me too

Scene 20

Instagram #6

LILY makes a video, her face staring straight into the camera, a forced smile.

LILY: Hey, friends—remember what they taught us in kinder-garten? "Do unto others as you would do unto yourself" #gandhi #bible #notsurewhichone. Would you want everyone talking about your private life? Gossip and rumours are for people with nothing better to do. Move on.

> LILY *stares at her phone for a moment, then deletes the video and starts another.* LILY *is almost shaking with anger while she films.*

Do any of you even have lives? Do you have nothing better to do than to gossip about a party that happened a week ago and spread rumours about some shit you didn't even see first-hand? Do you literally have nothing else to talk about? Why don't you all stop being assholes and focus on being actual good people. Is that too hard for you? Fuck you!

> LILY *exhales sharply, composes herself, then hits delete. She puts the phone back in her pocket. She struggles to compose herself, paces back and forth, maybe cries and/or has trouble breathing. At the peak of her anxiety, she takes a picture of herself—no duckface, just real. She looks at it for a moment. She doesn't know what to think. She puts her phone back in her pocket.*

Scene 21

The "R" Word

> LILY *and* EMMA *in a hallway at school.*

EMMA: Hey.

LILY: Omigod hi, I've sent you like a million texts.

EMMA: I know, my mom is kind of—

LILY: Oh my god yeah, understandable.

EMMA: —so I just couldn't—

LILY: What's going on, are you okay?

EMMA: Yeah, I'm fine.

LILY: Are you? Like, what is up, dude?

EMMA: What do you mean?

LILY: I just mean like—I don't know what's going on, but I'm trying to help and I feel like you're like . . . not there. And I don't know how else I can tell you that you're really important to me, so like . . . yeah. If that makes sense.

EMMA: Yeah.

LILY: And like ever since you got back from Paris things have been weird. And now this, and everything. And with everything going on, I mean I like honestly don't want to make it about me, I honestly don't, but just . . . um, yeah.

EMMA: I know. I'm sorry. I uh, I guess I've been kind of a shitty friend, in a way.

LILY: No, not at all, it's just—

EMMA: Well, actually, yeah, kinda. Um. I think, yeah, things have been kind of weird. Everything happened so fast. And I feel kind of stuck. It's kind of funny that you say things have been weird since I got back from Paris, because actually I had a really shitty time in Paris.

LILY: Oh. It didn't look like you did.

EMMA: That was the point.

LILY: What about the warehouse party?

EMMA: I didn't go. My host family wanted to take me for dinner.

LILY: So?

EMMA: Well I wasn't going to just say no. But my group was supposed to text me later and tell me where the party was.

LILY: And?

EMMA: Well, I texted them but they never texted me back.

LILY: Rude!

EMMA: So I basically just sat there in my room all dressed up to go out, watching everyone post pictures on Instagram of their fun night.

LILY: Shit, dude.

EMMA: I guess just for once I didn't want to be the loser who ended up staying at home. I'm so, so sick of it. So I just took a picture of myself, posted it. Who would know? I just thought maybe if it looked like I had this epic summer it would feel like I really did. It's stupid. I don't know why I did it.

LILY: Woah.

EMMA: So you didn't have to worry about me changing or whatever because maybe I'm just exactly the same as I always was.

LILY: Well how was I supposed to know? Why didn't you just tell me?

EMMA: I just thought maybe—I don't even know. I don't even know what I was thinking. I just wanted to feel like I could . . . well, it doesn't matter.

LILY: I guess I sounded like an idiot then, being so worried.

EMMA: No. It made me feel like . . . yeah, like you said, that I'm important to you. I just wish I had been more respectful of that. I'm sorry that I left it so long.

LILY: Yeah. I'm glad you told me.

Pause.

EMMA: So, uh, it's just a lot right now. I just don't know what to do. I don't know what to say. And now I have to do another police interview, and I'm just feeling like I don't want to—I don't know how much longer I can—I'm just so scared, Lily. I'm so scared and I just want to make it all go away, but I can't, but I just have to— / I *need* you, Lily.

LILY: I know, I'm so sorry that this is happening. I know things are all, like, messed up and scary now, and I don't want to, like, stress you out or anything, but people are starting to figure out that you're the one who went to the police.

EMMA: Oh god.

LILY: And the questions they're asking the guys—I mean, they're asking them what girls they were with that night. I mean everyone knows what they're investigating—

EMMA: Shit.

LILY: —basically that you said something happened, and that there's some, like, creeper out there. And like—it's a scary misunderstanding and it's horrible, but we can get it under control. You just have to be really careful about what you say.

EMMA: What do you mean?

LILY: Well like—people don't know you and Chris are a thing. No one saw you together. So you can just say you don't know who it was.

EMMA: Lily—

LILY: Just listen to me—obviously they've just *decided* what happened to you, so you have to be careful not to get Chris in trouble.

EMMA: What?

LILY: Dude, it's okay, I promise. It's just a misunderstanding. Some doctor overreacted, but you're the one who knows the truth. That nothing bad happened.

EMMA: But that's not the truth.

Beat.

LILY: What?

EMMA: I don't know.

LILY: No, what?

EMMA: I mean like. What happened. Wasn't good.

LILY: Okay, if you go in there saying stuff like this, they're going to get the wrong idea—

EMMA: What does that even mean, the wrong idea?

LILY: You're going to make it sound like Chris raped you.

Beat.

EMMA tries to speak but cannot. But she holds her ground.

Beat.

Are you fucking kidding me right now? Like, listen to the actual words you are saying right now. Are you insane? I mean like you're talking about *Chris* right now—

EMMA: Please, please don't do this. This is what I was scared—

LILY: You can't say anything about Chris. You can't tell them anything bad happened.

EMMA: I get to decide.

LILY: You just have to say that you were confused but everything is fine and then it will go away.

EMMA: Not for me.

LILY: What is your problem, Emma?

EMMA: My problem is that I woke up not knowing what happened to me and not remembering anything—

LILY: And you're being *honest* with me?

EMMA: What?

LILY: I mean you made up this fantasy trip in Paris, fake fucking warehouse parties.

EMMA: That's different.

LILY: Yeah, because this is, like, so real. Go ahead, tell the police whatever story you want, but don't punish Chris for nothing. You make it sound like he's some violent psychopath and he's not, and everyone knows that. So did / you actually tell the doctor that—

EMMA: It's complicated—

LILY: No, it's not, it's pretty fucking simple. You were at a party. You *danced* with him, you *kissed* him. So yeah, you got too drunk to remember what you did, but *you did it*. I mean, come on, you know Chris, my BROTHER, you know he's not a monster / or-or a criminal—

EMMA: / I know that—

LILY: Then why are you saying this?

EMMA: Because it's the truth.

LILY: So we're only doing truths now?

EMMA: Only truths now.

LILY: Okay.

Scene 22

Instagram #7

A picture of EMMA *and* CHRIS *kissing in the hallway. Blurry filter.*

LILY: #truelove

Scene 23

Comment Storm #3

A flood of comments from dozens of people. The text appears on the screens behind them.

CHRIS: UMMM

LILY: hang on

EMMA: what?

CHRIS: I thought she called the cops

LILY: She did

EMMA: She was talking about Chris?

CHRIS: she likes him?

LILY: she always did

EMMA: oh my god

LILY: she loves him

CHRIS: woah, it was Chris?!

EMMA: she's obsessed

LILY: but they're like making out

EMMA: that doesn't mean anything—

CHRIS: why is she getting mad now?

EMMA: wtf is this

LILY: you can't just say stuff like that about someone

CHRIS: ya you can't just ruin someone's life

EMMA: he's a good guy

LILY: I don't care, that's so fucked up if it's true

CHRIS: but why would she want to get him in trouble

EMMA: we don't know all the facts—

LILY: fucking liar

CHRIS: ohhh wowww #METOO

EMMA: fucking slut

CHRIS: wow

LILY: rude

EMMA: bitch

CHRIS / EMMA / LILY: poor chris

EMMA: she better watch herself

Scene 24

The Story

EMMA, CHRIS, and LILY speak to the audience.

LILY: Do you ever just wanna

EMMA: Delete

CHRIS: Delete

LILY: Delete

EMMA: Oops

CHRIS: Never mind

LILY: My bad

EMMA: Clean slate

CHRIS: New start

LILY: Fresh page

EMMA: Just me

CHRIS: Me

LILY: Me

EMMA: The real me

CHRIS: Whoever that is

LILY: But once you hit send

EMMA: It's there

CHRIS: It's real

LILY: Whatever real means

EMMA: And you can't take it back

CHRIS: No matter what

LILY: Is that really true?

EMMA: All I know is

CHRIS: All I want is

LILY: All I need is

EMMA: To go back

CHRIS: That night

LILY: That party

EMMA: Can I rewrite the story?

CHRIS / LILY: So there's a party

CHRIS: And everyone shows up

LILY: We do some shots

CHRIS: We take some pictures

LILY: And everyone has fun

CHRIS: We have some drinks

LILY: We dance

CHRIS: We talk

LILY: I hit the lights

CHRIS: And I kiss her in the dark

LILY: He tells her something important

CHRIS: I hold her hand

LILY: And that's it

CHRIS: That's all

LILY: The end

EMMA: No.

The lights snap down on LILY and CHRIS.

There is no end. Even if I rewrote the story from the beginning. I've probably tried a thousand times. Sitting in class, lying in bed, riding the bus, I'm back there, I'm back in the sweat and the music, his hands on my waist, holding hands in the dark. I'm there. The party. And I think, what if ... what if ...

But there is no end. Because I always come back. And I'm at the hospital or in the principal's office or staring at my phone while a million messages come up on my screen calling me a slut and a liar. You can't rewrite it. And there is no end. No matter how much you want it.

I wonder what happens next? Maybe the police find the picture and arrest Chris at soccer practice and throw him in jail. Maybe they say they've made a mistake and they let us both go. Maybe nobody believes me and they call me a liar for the rest of my life.

I take one last look at my Instagram, my Facebook, my Snapchat, and ... delete. Goodbye to the Eiffel Tower and my face, dressed up for a party I never went to. Goodbye to the summer at the cottage where I fell in love for the first time. Goodbye to three best friends, sweaty and drunk at a party. Goodbye to the most precious, the most private moment of my life up there for everyone to see. Goodbye. Delete.

I can't rewrite my story, but neither can anyone else. It was true when I was too scared to admit it. It was true when no one would listen. My story was always there.

My story. The truth.

Scene 25

Selfie

Outside, late. CHRIS and EMMA.

CHRIS: Hey, sorry I'm late.

EMMA: No, no that's okay.

Beat.

CHRIS: I'm kinda lucky. They cancelled practice today so I had the night off. I was glad—when you called me. That I could.

EMMA: Ah.

CHRIS: My dad doesn't really—Lily and I are kind of on lockdown because of the party.

EMMA: Right.

CHRIS: And you're allowed . . . ?

EMMA: Sort of. I told my mom I just really needed some time alone. She trusts me, so.

CHRIS: That's good.

EMMA: And she doesn't have Facebook or Instagram or anything, so she won't see the picture for, like, two weeks, haha.

CHRIS: Oh, um. Yeah.

EMMA: It's okay, I've seen it. And what people said.

CHRIS: It's really really fucked up.

EMMA: I don't really care, to be honest.

CHRIS: Really?

EMMA: Yeah. Somehow, really.

CHRIS: What do you think is gonna happen? When the cops find it?

EMMA: I have no idea.

They sit for a while.

CHRIS: I hate this. I really hate this.

EMMA: Yep.

CHRIS: Like right now I hate everyone at school, and I hate the cops, and I hate the counsellors, and I hate myself more than anyone else. I just don't understand how we got here. How everything is so fucked up.

EMMA just watches CHRIS.

I was thinking about stuff. And about how long I wanted to be with you. Lily told me that you didn't think I liked you. And I was like, why? And she said its 'cause I always acted like a loser around you. And I guess Lily's definition of "loser" is that I was quiet and stuff, but that's because I was trying NOT to be a loser.

I just always imagined—I don't know, that one day we'd be alone and I would just have the right thing to say. Like, just out of nowhere. But I never did so I just didn't really say anything. So stupid. So fucking stupid.

And now, like—everyone is looking at this picture of, like, the actual best moment of my life. And, like, they're all fucking judging it and—

Well, like, not the best moment of my life. But it would have been. It, like, should have been. Like any other time it would have been just the happiest thing in the whole world.

Fuck, I don't know what I'm saying.

I'm just talking.

Sorry.

EMMA: Yeah. It would have been really nice.

CHRIS: But it can't be now?

EMMA: No.

CHRIS: Okay.

They sit for a while.

EMMA: I used to imagine being with you too.

CHRIS: Yeah?

EMMA: I kind of imagined . . . it's stupid.

CHRIS: You're never stupid.

EMMA: I had this vision that, like, at the end of the party after everyone left, there would be like a huge mess. Pineapple under the couch.

They laugh.

And everyone would just leave, and no one would offer to stay and help, and Lily would be, like, passed out or too lazy to help.

CHRIS: Sounds about right.

EMMA: And maybe you'd be all stressed out 'cause your parents were coming home in the morning. But I would be there to help you. And I'd stay until everything was cleaned up, till it was really really early in the morning. We'd be really tired so we'd just sit on the couch together, and then fall asleep.

CHRIS: Perfect.

EMMA: Yeah. Oh well.

CHRIS: But we still could. I mean, I don't know what's going to happen with the picture and the police and everyone but just like—just now. We could just sit here. It could be like that, just for a second.

EMMA: *(gently)* No, Chris.

CHRIS: Yeah. Yeah, you're right.

Pause.

I love you.

Pause.

EMMA: What?

CHRIS: I've been in love with you for like a year. I told you at the party.

EMMA: Oh.

CHRIS: You really don't remember anything?

EMMA: I don't.

CHRIS: Okay. I mean, I know you told me that before, but I didn't know it was so . . .

EMMA: Yeah. Pretty scary.

CHRIS: I'm sorry.

EMMA: Why are you sorry?

CHRIS: Because . . . because all this stuff.

EMMA: What stuff?

CHRIS: I don't know.

EMMA: What stuff? What stuff are you talking about?

CHRIS: Like the picture, and—

EMMA: No. No. You know what I'm talking about. You know what I'm talking about. You told me you loved me, okay, but that's not it. That's not it.

CHRIS: I'm sorry.

EMMA: Don't tell me you're sorry. Don't say that you're sorry when you don't even know what you're saying sorry for.

CHRIS: For everything.

EMMA: For what? For what? Why can't you say it?

CHRIS: I don't know.

EMMA: You do!

CHRIS: I fucked up! I did fuck up. Like I always do. I messed up our first time together. If I knew you wouldn't remember I would never have done it. I'm sorry, I'm so, so sorry.

EMMA: But it's not just—

LILY enters, running.

LILY: What's going on?

CHRIS: Lily, go home.

LILY: No fucking way. I tried to call you but you didn't answer, so I just looked, okay? And I saw your car parked in the lot and also you guys are yelling at each other.

CHRIS: / We weren't yelling—

EMMA: No one is yelling—

LILY: Emma, I didn't know you'd be here. I am so sorry. I didn't know people would freak out—

CHRIS: You completely fucked me over, too.

EMMA: What did you think was going to happen?

LILY: I just thought—I don't know, not that. I thought people would just be like—

CHRIS: What the fuck were you thinking?

EMMA: But why did you do it?

LILY: I just thought—I just thought if you were going to say something to the police about Chris, that at least people would know that you . . . that you were together. That you wanted to be together.

CHRIS: What were you going to say?

EMMA: I hadn't decided anything, / I just—

LILY: Well that's not what it sounded like. And I guess I freaked out. But I already deleted it.

CHRIS: What were you going to say?

LILY: It's fucked, what people were saying. It's totally fucked.

EMMA: Well thanks for deleting it, but it's too late.

LILY: Okay. I'm sorry.

EMMA: I don't really need to hear anyone tell me they're sorry again. It doesn't really help.

LILY: Well what are we supposed to say?

Beat.

It was just a party. I just—I just thought I was doing a good thing for my brother and my friend. I mean—I mean, seriously, what the hell is going on? You're my best friends. We can't be like this . . . Emma, you are *always* there and you're always kind and smart, and you always have the right things to say and I can't lose that in my life. Please, Emma! I love you. I was so wrong and I messed up, okay? I totally messed up, but I didn't mean to and I can fix it and I'm so, so sorry—

EMMA: Calm down.

LILY: Don't be mad at me. Please please don't be mad at me—I just wanted us to all stay together—

CHRIS: SHUT UP, Lily, just SHUT UP.

LILY: *(quietly)* Okay. Okay fine.

Pause.

CHRIS: What were you going to say to the police?

EMMA: I don't know. I don't know what to say.

CHRIS: Look, I . . . I didn't know. I didn't know you wouldn't remember. It wasn't right. I had this feeling . . . but I just wanted to so much and—even after the party I thought maybe it was okay, but now I know you really didn't remember—

EMMA: But that's not it.

Beat.

I didn't want to have sex.

Pause.

CHRIS: You didn't want to?

EMMA: I would have said no if I knew what was happening.

CHRIS: Oh my god. Oh my god.

He paces.

I'm going to throw up.

He turns around quickly, coughs a bit, but doesn't throw up. Shakily he sits on the ground.

(quietly) I fuck things up. I always fuck things up. Everyone thinks I'm so good but I'm not.

Pause.

LILY: Emma? *(intention: is that true?)*

EMMA: Yeah.

EMMA nods.

Yeah.

LILY: Fuck.

EMMA: Why did you even take that picture?

LILY: I saw you in the hall, and—I was—I was just happy for you that you were getting together.

EMMA: You were there.

LILY: I just came up to check on you.

EMMA: Why?

LILY: Because you were really drunk.

EMMA: And you just walked away?

LILY stands for a long moment. She turns to CHRIS.

LILY: Stand up, Chris. Stand. Up.

CHRIS struggles to his feet.

CHRIS: But I didn't—I didn't mean to hurt you. I would never hurt you—

EMMA: You did hurt me.

CHRIS: But like . . . I don't understand. I don't understand. I just wanted to be with you. I mean, we were dancing, *you kissed me*—

EMMA: I was so drunk.

CHRIS: Me too.

EMMA: Yeah, I kissed you, but I can barely remember anything after that—

CHRIS: Fuck—

Beat.

I just . . . I would never. That's not who I am. I would never.

EMMA: But you did. You did, but I'm the one who . . . and I don't care that you didn't mean to hurt me because I hurt so much, and I hurt inside and out and now everyone—everyone—knows about it and I'm stuck here.

CHRIS: Tell me what to do. Tell me how to fix it.

EMMA: You can't fix it. You can't take it back. This *happened*. I *trusted* you.

CHRIS: Sorry.

EMMA: What does that matter now? What does it matter? It happened. To *me*. Not to you, not to Lily. Me. And I don't give a shit if you meant to or didn't mean to and I don't give a shit what everyone else thinks. I know that . . . I know. I *know*. Even if I'm all alone in that.

LILY: You're not alone. You're not. I'm here. Emma . . .

She reaches out to EMMA.

I'm here.

EMMA looks at her for a moment and then hugs her. They hold each other for a while—maybe LILY whispers in EMMA's ear— then part. While this is happening, CHRIS says, softly:

CHRIS: I'm so sorry.

A long pause. LILY *looks over at* CHRIS *standing apart from them, and then back to* EMMA.

LILY: What do we do now?

EMMA: I don't know.

Scene 26

Breathe

EMMA: When it all began, I felt like I was underwater, deep below, like when you jump from a diving board. The pressure of the water held me tightly, pressing in on my skin. It was dark, and all I could hear was the roar of the water around me. But I had forgotten that I could float. Now I'm rushing towards the surface, lungs burning from holding my breath, knowing in just a few seconds I'll make it.

There's the temptation to give in, to take that desperate breath my instincts tell me I need. There are days where the pain is so intense that I wonder if it's easier to just breathe in, let the water take me.

But I hold on—I hold on.

I'm feeling the water loosen its grip, feeling the sun grow hotter as I move closer and closer to the surface.

I can almost breathe again. I'm almost there.

EMMA looks out at the audience, standing alone on stage.

Afterword

What happens next?

In almost every post-show talkback of *Selfie*, what happens next is a vigorous defence of Chris. His innocence gets discussed, how unfair his treatment is, how dire his future seems now. At times, I (the playwright) am accused of creating propaganda that demonizes men and boys. In the words of a review from a Vancouver production: "I get it. It's rape. But, damn, when a sixteen or seventeen-year-old girl chugalugs tequila straight from the bottle, agrees to go to a boy's bedroom and then passes out, perhaps there should be allowances made for an eighteen-year-old guy—also pretty drunk—who takes advantage of the opportunity?" Emma's trauma and harm become an afterthought.

I know why that is the response to *Selfie*. That response is why I wrote this piece. Our society is excellent at condemning sexual assault. We're very, very bad at condemning the perpetrators, or even just the circumstances and intentions of their actions. It's very easy to separate the people we know from the Brock Turners of the world. It's not easy to do so with characters that resemble our siblings, our children, our partners. Make no mistake—each of us knows and loves more Chrises than Brocks.

So what happens next then?

This is a work of fiction. Though it is drawn from real-life cases both high-profile and close to home, the characters and scenarios are not real. So we can do what we cannot do in real life—go back to the beginning and learn from how woefully unprepared these three young people are to handle themselves in the practice of consent. In the words of a young man in a Toronto talkback: "Everyone tells us to use consent, but no one will tell us what that actually means." How do we fail young people with our inability to teach what consensual interaction sounds and looks like? How do we carry those failures forward and propagate them in our adult lives?

Behind the defence of Chris is our fear—our fear that our children may one day be perpetrators, that we ourselves have been perpetrators, that the failures of our social systems have resulted in an untrusting and wounded public that has turned to vigilante actions to receive justice. If we can transform that fear into deep compassion for all three of these young people, we can begin to heal the wounds of a culture with deep, deep damage around consent, sexual assault, and justice. We can honour survivors of sexual assault through creating a healthier culture by educating ourselves and our community. We can change not the ending, but the beginning.

I wrote this play out of deep love for all three characters, and for every young person navigating our damaged culture. I wrote this play to give voice to the fear and shame we carry with us, the violence we are capable of, and with the hope of starting the conversations that always come too late.

With that, I leave you with a few discussion prompts:

- What is consent?
- List as many infractions of consent in the play as you can find.
- What do you wish the characters had known?
- What do you wish you knew?
- How can you practise consent in your daily life?

Acknowledgements

This play was first written on the unceded, traditional, and unsurrendered territories of the Musqueam, Squamish, and Tsleil-Waututh people.

With great thanks to the many friends who read and listened to the various drafts of *Selfie* over the years (and my anxious ramblings about said drafts); to Jiv for his love and support; to Craig Holzschuh, whose initial commission and leap of faith changed my life; to Stephen Colella for taking the cold submission I stuffed in his YPT mailbox and making the play into what it is today; to Rachel and Marcus for their early support; to Colin Rivers for being a champion of my writing; to Rachel, Chris, Caroline, Siona, Vincent, and Julie for their courage in performance and in discussion; and to the many people who shared their stories with me to shape this one.

Born in Los Angeles to a Mexican American father and a Dutch British Canadian mother, Christine Quintana is now a grateful visitor on the unceded territories of the Musqueam, Squamish, and Tsleil-Waututh nations. Other playwriting highlights include *Never The Last* (co-created with Molly MacKinnon), winner of a Significant Artistic Achievement Award. Christine is a Siminovitch Prize Protégé winner for playwriting and is currently playwright-in-residence at Tarragon Theatre. She is a proud founding member of the Canadian Latinx Theatre Artist Coalition and holds a BFA in Acting from UBC.

First edition: November 2020
Printed and bound in Canada by Rapido Books, Montreal

Jacket art by Katie So

**PLAYWRIGHTS
CANADA PRESS**
202-269 Richmond St. w.
Toronto, ON
M5V 1X1

416.703.0013
info@playwrightscanada.com
www.playwrightscanada.com
@playcanpress